Original title:
The Porch That Heals

Copyright © 2025 Creative Arts Management OÜ
All rights reserved.

Author: Thomas Sinclair
ISBN HARDBACK: 978-1-80587-142-2
ISBN PAPERBACK: 978-1-80587-612-0

Where Breathe Meets Breeze

In the corner, a chair does creak,
Underneath, the grass plays hide and seek.
A sandwich flies by on its daring quest,
While a squirrel looks on, thinking it's best.

The sunbeams dance like a joyful jester,
As laugh tracks echo from each wild tester.
Here all concerns seem to fade and wane,
Even the worries play hide-and-seek in the grain.

Reflections on a Rustic Swing

Swinging back and forth, oh what a ride,
Birds circle 'round, taking it all in stride.
A glass with ice clinks, what could be better?
Except the neighbor's cat tangled in the sweater.

With every push, the world seems to laugh,
A bee buzzes by, trying to steal my half.
Moments like these tickle the spirit's dream,
Where nothing is serious, or so it seems.

Heartstrings in the Open Air

Heartstrings pluck in our summer song,
As bugs join in, proving they belong.
A breeze comes by, with laughter it shares,
While I trip on my shoes, oh the woes and glares!

In the distance, a harmonica cries,
Against the laughter of passing flies.
Amidst the giggles and mischief we weave,
Life's a comedy, if you dare to believe.

Serenity at the Threshold

At the edge of magic, the butterflies play,
With giggles echoing throughout the day.
Toes in the grass, feeling so free,
A sunbeam trips over, shouting 'look at me!'

Whispers of joy dance in the air,
As the wind tells secrets that others won't share.
Time pauses here with a chuckle and grin,
Even the clouds puff up with a mischievous spin.

Melodies of Solitude Underfoot

In a corner where shadows dance,
My cat plots mischief, given the chance.
The floor creaks like an old folk song,
Echoing tales of what feels wrong.

Chairs tell secrets, worn and torn,
While dust bunnies leap, all forlorn.
A mug of tea, my trusted friend,
As I scribble thoughts that never end.

Where Heartache Meets Harmony

A sock on the floor, a mismatched pair,
Lamenting the love lost in thin air.
But with every sip of homemade brew,
I find my rhythm, all's not so blue.

Laughter bubbles like a boiling pot,
As I trip on the rug and forget what I sought.
The melody of life is silly and bright,
In the chaos, I dance, everything's right.

An Oasis of Connection

Neighbors yell over fences and walls,
Their own serenade of weekend brawls.
I wave a hand as I sip on my fizz,
This social life? A hilarious whizz!

The plants all gossip about passerby,
While I sit, sipping lemonade, oh my!
You'd think they'd chat about the weather instead,
But it's all about Mr. Frisky and his cat bed.

Warmth of the Setting Sun

The sun dips low, a golden sneak,
And I tripped on my own two feet, so bleak!
But laughter erupts, a giggle or two,
As my shadow dances, just like I do.

The chase of fireflies begins anew,
A flicker of light, oh, that will do!
With nature's jokes and a warm embrace,
Who needs perfection in this silly space?

Shadows of the Past

In the corner, a chair that squeaks,
And tales of mishaps fill the weeks.
With every creak, a giggle is found,
As ghosts of my youth dance all around.

Laughter erupts from an old, worn rug,
Where my brother once tripped and hugged a bug.
We reminisce on the wild and wacky,
And that time Mom lost her purse—so tacky!

Visions of Tomorrow

Sipping tea while the sun takes a bow,
Dreams of what's next, oh where and how?
A future so bright, with laughs and more,
Maybe we'll start a lemonade store.

The visions are grand, but wait, oh dear,
What if our recipe's the cause of fear?
A lemon gone rogue, a taste quite bizarre,
But hey, we might just become rockstars!

Solace Within Wooden Beams

Nestled between the beams that creak,
I find laughter in chaos, so bleak.
A squirrel darts by, in search of his stash,
While I share my deep thoughts in a loud crash.

Worries take flight like leaves in the breeze,
Each giggle brings calm, like a gentle tease.
Here, warmth surrounds like a worn-out quilt,
As humor and joy together are built.

The Healing Hearth of Evening

As stars twinkle like shiny bling,
We gather 'round, and let joy take wing.
A fire crackles, roasting faux marshmallows,
And dad's bad jokes? They're for the gallows!

Each chuckle ignites the night so bright,
While shadows dance in the cheerful light.
Cousins compete for the funniest tale,
With punchlines that never, ever fail.

Tales in the Twilight Glow

In twilight's embrace, stories unfold,
With mishaps and memories, laughter's gold.
A misfit cat joins our festive chat,
Knocking down cups, wearing a hat!

We share our dreams, as silly as pie,
While debating if ducks can really fly.
With giggles and grins, the night drapes low,
In this sacred space, let the laughter flow.

The Embrace of Twilight

As dusk approaches with a smile,
I sit and watch the day beguile.
Squirrels dance in silly chase,
One trips and lands with quite a grace.

The sky is painted purple hues,
While fireflies jiggle, sharing news.
A neighbor's cat makes quite a scene,
Chasing shadows on the green.

Old dogs snooze, dreaming of snacks,
While kids plan their evening hacks.
Laughter rings beneath the stars,
Imagination takes us far.

In twilight's arms, we find our cheer,
Lost in tales that we hold dear.
Time stops for shenanigans bright,
In the calm embrace of night.

Where Shadows Gather Light

Underneath the old oak tree,
Shadows whisper, come and see.
A raccoon sneaks, all too sly,
With a twinkle in his eye.

Granny's rocking chair creaks anew,
As the breeze sings softly too.
A toad croaks jokes to beetle pals,
While everyone avoids the quails.

Silly bugs in fancy dress,
Buzzing round in wild excess.
The stars peek out, a merry sight,
Making fun of the fading light.

In this realm where shadows play,
Joy and laughter lead the way.
We gather tales like firefly glow,
In whispers soft, our spirits grow.

Healing Breezes at Dusk

The evening breeze tickles my nose,
As silly thoughts begin to pose.
A leaf drops down, gives me a wink,
I swear it knows more than I think!

A cat strolls by, looking quite wise,
With swagger as big as the skies.
She stops and yawns, then strikes a pose,
Like she's the queen of all that grows.

Fireflies light up their own show,
Turning the yard into a glow.
A crow cackles from a nearby fence,
I chuckle, wondering about his sense.

In healing breezes, joy takes flight,
With every chuckle, the world feels right.
So here I sit, beneath the moon,
Cracking jokes with the stars in tune.

Conversations with the Wind

The wind whispers secrets, soft and light,
Floats through my hair, a playful flight.
I ask it questions, it answers back,
With giggles that echo, just off track.

It swirls around like a silly friend,
Telling tales that never end.
Like a kite on strings, it dances away,
In laughter and breeze, we twist and play.

Leaves erupt in a rustling cheer,
As the wind winks, drawing near.
A squirrel rolls by, acting absurd,
Chasing whispers, not a word heard.

In this chat with the merry gust,
I find my heart learns to trust.
With each silly tale and howling breath,
The wind reminds me there's no death.

Lullabies of the Leaving Light

As sun dips low and shadows play,
The garden gnomes start their ballet.
A cat in shades, shades of flair,
Watches squirrels with a curious stare.

The hummingbird sips afternoon tea,
With stories about an old apple tree.
A breeze whispers secrets quite absurd,
As daisies giggle, their heads all stirred.

In the dusk, a frog out on the log,
Croaks a tune much like a fog.
Fireflies start their glow-in-the-dark,
While a hedgehog hums, lost in a spark.

Harmony in Stillness

The chairs squeak in a playful tune,
While crickets join in a late afternoon.
A dog snorts loud, dreaming of chase,
As the porch sways, a gentle embrace.

The old clock ticks, but jumps ahead,
Time's a tease, a featherbed.
A raccoon struts like it owns the place,
Causing all the flowers to lose their grace.

A cloud drifts by, wearing a grin,
While a snail races, though it's a sin.
A laughter rings out, echoing sweet,
As the sun bids farewell, tapping its feet.

The Space Between Moments

A cup of tea spills, a splash of cheer,
Ticklish breezes tickle the ear.
A squirrel stops, it's quite aloof,
In a tiny hat, sitting on a roof.

Wisps of clouds tickle the ground,
While toes wiggle, the grass profound.
In this magic nook of sunlight's play,
Even the shadows dance away.

Puddles reflect a topsy-world,
Where dreams and giggles are unfurled.
The world slows down just for a laugh,
As the moon winks, a cheeky half.

Footprints in the Dust of Time

Footprints scatter, stories to share,
Of cats and hats, all beyond compare.
A juggling mouse, quite out of place,
Leaves us giggling, a furry disgrace.

Dust bunnies plot their nightly schemes,
In the corners where sunlight beams.
A wandering frog, a tap dancer's fire,
Brings happy chaos, never to tire.

Time just giggles, bending and twirling,
In moments silly, like this world's whirling.
With laughter echoing through the years,
We dance with dust and chase our fears.

Connection to the Unseen

In the corner swings a chair,
My cat thinks it's her throne,
Watching squirrels dance around,
While I sip on lemonade alone.

Invisible friends drop by,
With stories from the past,
They crack jokes and laugh with me,
Though their visits never last.

A ghostly dog sits in the shade,
Barking at the mailman's side,
I chuckle at his antics wild,
With my laughter as my guide.

The sun dips low, a painted sky,
The day dances into night,
With every sip and silly thought,
I find joy in sheer delight.

Threads of Time in a Still Space

The rocking chair creaks with age,
A tale of all my years,
As I knit my thoughts in yarn,
And battle the passing years.

I once caught a fish so grand,
That tales were spun with ease,
But it was really just a shoe,
Loosely tied by the breeze.

My knitting needles dance and play,
Like tiny clapping hands,
Creating worlds of fuzzy warmth,
While my mind quietly expands.

Time drips slow like honey jar,
Sweet moments stick so tight,
Laughter bubbles from the past,
Illuminated by starlight.

Beneath the Open Sky

Underneath the big blue dome,
The clouds parade like sheep,
While I toast marshmallows bright,
And ponder things way too deep.

A chipmunk tried to take a nut,
But tripped on his own feet,
I laughed so hard, I nearly fell,
As nature matched my beat.

Sitting back on old lawn chairs,
I sipped iced tea with flair,
Talking to the passing ants,
Who were surprisingly rare.

The stars peek out, they wink and grin,
As if they know my name,
In the fabric of the evening sky,
Laughter's all the same.

The Soul's Quiet Harbor

A creaky bench holds many dreams,
With wooden arms that sway,
I rest my thoughts here lightly,
While colors brighten day.

My neighbor's dog gives me the eye,
As if he owns this space,
I share my snack without a care,
While he guards his furry grace.

Every laughter floated by,
Is captured for a while,
In whispers from the branches deep,
That sway with cheerful style.

The sunset's shades paint goofy flips,
As shadows start to hide,
I linger long to breathe it in,
And smile at the tide.

In the Nest of Calm

Sitting here with tea in hand,
Breezes dance like they have planned.
Birds gossip in the hazy light,
Guess they're working on their flight.

Cats nap in the sunlit rays,
Trusting shadows to replace their plays.
A squirrel tries to steal my snack,
He's bold but I'll just chase him back.

Neighbors laugh, they play charades,
"Who'll be the one to catch the spades?"
I'll just sit and watch it all,
Laughter's better when it's small.

The world can whirl, but here I'll stay,
Wrapped in giggles, come what may.
Beneath this roof, so calm, so grand,
Life is truly just unplanned.

The Stillness Between Thoughts

Moments pause in the gentle breeze,
Thoughts dance lightly, like falling leaves.
A fly buzzes, thinking he's grand,
But I'm the monarch of this land.

Neighbors holler, 'What's the fuss?'
Life feels like a great big bus.
Popcorn kernels in the air,
Who knew laughter grew from care?

Turtles hide, playing peek-a-boo,
While I muse on what I'll do.
Why fret when giggles here abound?
In silence, joy is often found.

Between my thoughts, a joke may sprout,
Life's absurd, there's no doubt.
Hold this moment, treat it right,
Kidding! Trust me, it's a sight.

Unbroken by the Night

Stars twinkle like they've lost their way,
Moon laughs softly, begging us to play.
Crickets strum their nightly song,
And fireflies dance, all night long.

Wishes flutter like tired wings,
As laughter is the best of things.
Who needs a dream when you've got fun?
We'll just giggle till we're done.

S'mores get sticky, but that's the way,
Chocolate smears make a perfect play.
Ghosts may lurk in tales we tell,
But truth is fun, and treats do swell.

So here we sit, weaving the thread,
In goofy tales, our hearts are fed.
Let the night smirk, we'll outshine,
Tomorrow comes, and all is fine.

Dancing Flames and Kindled Spirits

Fires crackle with a vibrant spark,
Laughter bounces, bright and dark.
Marshmallows roast, they toast a tale,
About the day and how we sail.

Flames flicker like a cat's playful paw,
What's that? A shadow? Oh, it's just my jaw!
Oops, I slipped! The grass is wet.
But laughter's here, no room for regret.

Friends join in, a merry crowd,
Too many stories, that's allowed!
Who told that joke about the cat?
"Oh wait, it was me!" Who's sure of that?

As twilight deepens, spirits soar,
With every chuckle, we want more.
At day's end, when all's aglow,
Funny moments always steal the show.

Embracing Moments

On a creaky chair, I sit with glee,
Sipping lemonade, feeling so free.
Mosquitoes dance like they own the place,
While I swat them away with a comical grace.

Neighbors whisper tales of my antics,
Silly with laughter, I'm their best prankster.
A cat nearby thinks it reigns supreme,
Chasing after shadows with a feline dream.

Carving Peace

In the sun's glow, I carve my throne,
Napping on cushions with a sleepy groan.
Birds start to chirp like they're in a band,
While I serenade with snacks at hand.

A squirrel hops by, a frantic little beast,
Stealing my chips, oh, what a feast!
I laugh and I chuckle at this furry thief,
Who's got a knack for comic relief.

Beneath the Canopy of Time.

Under a tree that knows my name,
I tell it secrets, it plays my game.
The wind joins in, a partner divine,
Rustling the leaves in a witty line.

Clouds drift above, like ships they float,
I wave at them, hoping they're note.
A sprinkle of rain joins the silly show,
Prompting my laughter to outgrow.

Whispers of Solace

With a book in hand and a quirk in my smile,
I dive in a story that lasts a while.
Characters dance like they've lost their way,
And I join their antics in a quirky play.

A breeze tugs at pages, oh what a tease!
As I chase them down with the greatest of ease.
Laughter erupts from the tales I embrace,
Turning my worries to a warmer place.

Serenity's Threshold

Swinging on swings that squeak and creak,
I ponder the cosmos, feel so unique.
The world spins by, a carnival ride,
While I sip moments with laughter as my guide.

Laughter echoes as my buddy joins in,
We role-play heroes, where do we begin?
A race to the finish, then falls in a heap,
While the stars become witnesses to our leap.

Solace Between the Lines

In the corner, a cat does stare,
As the wind tousles my hair.
A sandwich dropped, like a crime,
Seagulls gather, oh what a time!

The old chair squeaks, a familiar tune,
While laughter dances beneath the moon.
A lost shoe, who knows where it went?
The dog just grins, he's quite content.

A book half-read, I can barely recall,
Mismatched socks on a lazy sprawl.
Each page turns as I sip my tea,
Wondering what else could possibly be.

So here I sit, with no grand plans,
Just me, a snack, and some silly fans.
Life's absurd, yet here it glows,
In this moment, I've found my prose.

Moments of Clarity at Dusk

Sunset's glow paints skies so bright,
While mosquitoes take their nightly flight.
A tune from the fridge, oh what a fridge,
As I ponder if I should jump the ridge.

In the distance, a squirrel makes a dash,
While I sip lemonade, watching it splash.
What's that in my sandwich? A pickle?
My taste buds laugh, oh, what a trickle!

Laughter erupts from a neighboring yard,
While I workout with my trusty card.
Today's exercise? Just switch the chair!
A feat of epic, fresh air affair!

And as evening drapes its jeweled gown,
Moments of clarity chase the frown.
Grabbed my slippers, it's time to unwind,
In this little chaos, laughter I find.

The Calm in the Chaos

Amidst the noise, a bird seeks grace,
While I trip over my shoelace.
A bicycle wheel rolls by with glee,
And I wave back, "Hey, is that for me?"

The neighbor bakes, the smell's divine,
But then, oh dear, the smoke alarm whines.
Laughter bubbles as the tale unfolds,
In every mishap, joy behold!

My socks are mismatched, what a grand show,
While a dog demonstrates how to bellow.
Sunsets arrive, with colors that dance,
Amidst the mess, I take my chance.

So here I bask in this playful plight,
With moments that sparkle, pure delight.
Life's chaotic, but that's the catch,
In the calm, we find a perfect match.

Ferns and Footstools

Ferns in pots, green fronds aglow,
While I stumble, forgetting to go slow.
The footstool tips, a wild affair,
As I cling to laughter, backed by a chair.

Witty banter flows through the air,
As I juggle snacks without a care.
A sip of soda, a hiccup so loud,
With friends nearby, I feel so proud.

A cat jumps up, like a feathery sock,
And lands on the table, oh what a shock!
Yet we giggle and share in the jest,
These moments of joy, a true treasure chest.

So here's to ferns and memories spun,
To footstools and laughter, oh what fun!
In this quirky chaos, I find my peace,
A simple life, where laughter won't cease.

The Canvas of Quietude

On a canvas where silence waves,
Laughter hides in the curves it braves.
A squirrel snickers, a chipmunk twirls,
While butterflies spin in the quiet swirls.

A hammock sways with a creaky tune,
Sky spills colors like a sneeze from the moon.
Ticklish grass tickles your feet so bright,
Even the shadows giggle in delight.

Leaves whisper secrets, or so they say,
As clouds trip lightly, not one goes astray.
The sun has a chuckle, the breeze winks sly,
In this canvas, laughter flutters nearby.

So sit with me, let the world fade,
In this quiet wonder where joy's displayed.
For in every rustle, and every glance,
Lies a smile waiting to break into dance.

Serendipity Under Stars

Beneath a blanket of twinkling cheer,
Stars play hide-and-seek, never near.
A firefly winks with a cheeky grin,
While crickets buzz like they're about to win.

The moon's a jester in a silver hat,
Casting shadows where laughter's at.
A raccoon rummages, plotting its snack,
While a fox plays tag, gleefully back.

An owl's deep hoot is a punchline missed,
As the night unfolds, can you resist?
With every breath, the cosmos sighs,
Whispering secrets in starry ties.

So let us dance under laughter's light,
In the tapestry woven of sheer delight.
For every twinkle, a giggle found,
In this vast expanse where joys abound.

Embracing the Softness of Dusk

As daylight dips, a soft blush appears,
The sky tells stories, filled with cheers.
A lazy cat stretches, in sunlight's grace,
While the sun plays peek-a-boo, without a trace.

Crickets tune up, with a musical jive,
While fireflies practice, they're eager to thrive.
A gentle breeze whirls like it knows the beat,
Tickling the grass, oh what a treat!

Each corner holds laughter, unseen but near,
As the world exhales, shedding daily wear.
The twilight works magic, a playful disguise,
Where silliness reigns under artful skies.

So let's embrace this twilight delight,
In the softness of dusk, all feels just right.
For in each shadow, giggles abound,
In these tender moments, joy can be found.

Notes of Nature's Lullaby

In the orchestra of leaves, a soft tune plays,
A melody born of bright sunny days.
A woodpecker drums on a tree with glee,
While the breeze flutters by with a cheerful decree.

Fluttering butterflies write notes in the air,
Scripted in nectar, they dance without care.
The brook gurgles laughter, a bubbling spree,
As flowers nod gently, all grateful and free.

The sun dips low, casting shadows so wide,
While critters giggle, running to hide.
Nature hums softly, a lullaby sweet,
With every chirp, the earth finds its beat.

So rest in this symphony, let worries flee,
As you bask in nature's joyous decree.
For in every note, and every sway,
Lies a world of laughter, brightening the day.

Breath of the Evening Breeze

Evening air whispers tales of delight,
With dancing leaves, all spirits take flight.
A squirrel in a hat chases away the gloom,
While fireflies shimmer, shining up the room.

Laughter swirls like smoke from a fire,
The moon grins wide, lifting hearts higher.
A rocking chair creaks with a rhythmic cheer,
As crickets croon songs that only we hear.

Gentle Reflections of Life

In puddles of laughter, reflections abound,
Where daisies wear hats, buzzing bees spin around.
Sunsets giggle, painting skies bright,
While clouds take selfies, a whimsical sight.

A cat on a fence, with a bow tie no less,
Claims the best view of this evening's dress.
Smiles flow freely like lemonade's sweet cheer,
Reminding us all that life's good here.

Safe Haven from the Storm

When raindrops race, a comedic charade,
The roof hums a tune, like a serenade.
Wobbly chairs challenge, who can hold fast,
While popcorn pops loud, a party unsurpassed.

A dog dons a poncho, ready to play,
As thunder rolls in a comedic display.
Hot cocoa smiles from its mug warm and round,
In this joyous chaos, peace can be found.

Where Heart Meets Earth

On this patch of grass where giggles collide,
A dance with the daisies, come take a ride.
The sun winks at us, with a cheeky glow,
While ants host a picnic, just look at them go!

Tickles from breezes, the trees join the fun,
A swing sways gently, we're just on the run.
As shadows play tag with the fading light,
The earth cradles laughter, what a joyful sight!

The Language of the Stars

From rooftops high, the stars they squawk,
While squirrels debate in the evening shock.
What secrets they keep in their twinkling glow,
Must be about the snacks they're trading below.

The moon took a sip from a comet's tail,
And laughed at the sun as it told a tale.
Constellations gossip in a cosmic dance,
While owls roll their eyes at the firefly prance.

So when you gaze up at the blink and the flash,
Just know it's all part of the nightly bash.
They're not just stars, but the universe's jest,
How fun to imagine they're having a fest!

So grab a chair, under the night's embrace,
And laugh with the cosmos, it's a wondrous place.
Because in the sky, with its rambunctious crew,
Lies the joy of connection, both old and new.

Garden of Forgotten Dreams

In a garden where giggles sprout,
And flowers debate what life's about.
Each petal whispers a secret or two,
While weeds plot to steal the morning dew.

The daisies declare they're the queen of the scene,
While roses just pout, saying, 'We're too green!'
But laughter erupts from the paths of the night,
As dreams reemerge in the soft moonlight.

The gnomes hold court, sharing tales of old,
Of treasures and treasures, not just bought or sold.
They tip their hats as they wobble along,
In a garden where mischief plays all day long.

So slip off your shoes, let your worries fly,
In the garden where dreams never say goodbye.
For within every bloom is a memory bright,
That tickles your heart and ignites pure delight.

Fireside Revelations

By the fire, the logs chat with a crackle and pop,
Telling tales of the past, they can't seem to stop.
The shadows join in, doing their dance,
As marshmallows explode in a sugary trance.

The chair creaks a tune, asking for a story,
While socks claim they're the true seat of glory.
And yes, there's that one old blanket with flair,
That guarantees comfort beyond all compare.

The kettle joins in, singing a song,
Of tea leaves and gossip – oh, it won't be long.
As laughter spills over and whispers ignite,
The fireside becomes a cozy delight.

So gather around, let the warmth pull you near,
For the best kind of magic is laughter, my dear.
In these flickering moments, our hearts truly glow,
And after tonight, we'll be best friends, you know!

The Lightness of Being

When tickled by breezes, we float like a feather,
With dreams like balloons, all light as a tether.
Jumping through puddles, our shadows may kneel,
As giggles take flight with a magical feel.

The sun wears a grin, and clouds play their part,
As butterflies swoosh in a whimsical chart.
"Who knew being happy was such a delight?"
Cried the rabbit who danced with a rooster that night.

With each awkward twirl, and each silly fall,
We laugh at the tumble - oh, we'll still stand tall!
For every small slip, we find there's a prize,
In the lightness of joy that twinkles our eyes.

So let's frolic like children till daylight is wan,
For the world can be silly as we carry on.
In the joy of the moment, we finally see,
The secret to living is being so free!

Nature's Bounty of Peace

In the garden, weeds do dance,
A squirrel steals my only chance.
With bird songs fresh, I take a seat,
And trip on roots beneath my feet.

Flowers bloom, yet bees just buzz,
They'll steal my drink, or give me fuzz.
The sun rays flirt, they play so bold,
Am I the flower, or just the mold?

A lazy cat sprawls, soaking sun,
In this chaos, life's a pun.
The trees a-whisper of tall tales,
While I sip tea, my laugh prevails.

Nature's laughter, wild and free,
Turns my frown to a glee spree.
With every tick of the clock's 'tock',
I find my joy, not just in talk.

Raindrops and Reflections

Pitter patter on my hat,
A dance party beneath that sprat.
The puddles show my silly grin,
As I splash down, let fun begin!

Umbrellas up like blooming flowers,
A rain dance shared for hours and hours.
But oh, that bus, it goes right by,
Wet socks and laughter, oh my, oh my!

Each drop a friend that's come to play,
Are they dissolving all my gray?
I try to dodge the dripping fare,
But laugh instead, without a care!

Reflecting rainbows off my nose,
With muddy shoes, my joy just grows.
In every glisten, a giggle hides,
As nature's whimsy gently glides.

The Comfort of Familiar Skies

Above my head, those clouds, they tease,
Like cotton candy, they drift with ease.
I wonder if they'll drop their weight,
To rain down sprinkles and celebrate!

The sun will peek, a curious cat,
And warm my cheeks, imagine that!
When shadows stretch and dance about,
I chase them down and twist about.

The moon will wink, a cheeky sprite,
And throw some stars to spark the night.
With constellations on parade,
I muse on dreams, a little unmade.

In this vast sky, I find my seat,
With jokes and jests, it's quite a treat.
It's a familiar, cozy sight,
Where laughter lingers, and wrong feels right.

Embracing the Evening Glow

As dusk unravels, colors blend,
A playful breeze whispers, 'Come, my friend.'
The crickets sing, a goofy choir,
While fireflies dance in twinkly attire.

I settle down with snacks galore,
What's life without some marshmallow lore?
The sunset paints my world in glee,
With hues so bright, they shout at me!

Laughter echoes through the trees,
While nature hums her quirky tease.
With parked-up chairs and tales to tell,
The evening fills my heart so well.

Embracing moments, cheeky and light,
I welcome stars, the ones that bite.
And in this glow, I find my way,
Through silly thoughts that make me stay.

Sunlit Days and Starry Evenings

A hammock sways, a cat's in flight,
Chasing sunbeams, what a sight!
Sipping lemonade, spills on the floor,
Laughter echoes, we all want more.

Jokes about socks and their missing mates,
Witty banter while it dissipates.
Fireflies flicker, the night draws near,
We trip on bugs, but who has fear?

Sunrise giggles wake the day,
Cheerful moments come what may.
Whimsical thoughts in a curious dance,
We toast to life, we take a chance.

Moonlit vibes and playful wishes,
We feast on dreams and funny dishes.
Embracing joy with every quirk,
Life's silly moments, our favorite perk.

The Art of Letting Go

Tossing worries like a frisbee wide,
Letting them soar, we take it in stride.
Burdened by chores? We say, "Not today!"
We'd rather lounge and hide away.

A rubber chicken and a silly hat,
Chasing away woes with a playful chat.
Falling with laughter, we tumble and roll,
Finding our peace in a giggling stroll.

The laundry piles up, let it wait,
We'll dance on socks, it feels so great!
With friends beside us, fears in tow,
Crafting our fun, it's the way to go.

Erasers on hands mean we all are giddy,
Life's too short to be serious or gritty.
Embrace the chaos, love the mess,
Finding the light through joy, no less.

Healing Hues of Dusk

As twilight dances, colors collide,
Pink and orange take us for a ride.
In the sky, serenades play loud,
We wave to the stars, feeling quite proud.

A sassy breeze tickles our cheeks,
While we wait for laughter, a moment peaks.
Chasing fireflies, oh, what a race,
Stumbling and giggling, it's our happy place.

Whispers of crickets, a soothing sound,
Belly laughs echo, joy rebound.
We lean back, let worries prepare,
The colors of dusk brush off our care.

Glances exchanged, like lightning strikes,
In this twilight, everything spikes.
We share funny tales, let the moon glow,
In this vivid light, we feel the flow.

Contemplation at the Edge of Day

Sitting on steps, where the world unfolds,
Daydreaming tales with a twist so bold.
Tangled up thoughts, like spaghetti strands,
We laugh together, new journeys planned.

A squirrel steals snacks, what a sly rogue,
Chasing his shadow, he's lost in the fog.
Mismatched socks and a cup of tea,
Life's little quirks are what set us free.

The sun takes a bow, paints the sky bright,
While we snicker at clouds in flight.
Each sigh a giggle, each pause a perk,
Finding humor in life's crazy work.

Contemplating joy as day bids adieu,
With each laugh, our spirits renew.
Together we cherish, these simple displays,
Life's funny moments, the heart always sways.

Solitude's Resting Place

On a chair that squeaks and groans,
My thoughts wander like lost drones.
A cat naps on my silent lap,
While squirrels plot a daring cap.

The sunbeams dance, a golden twist,
I sip my drink, won't shake my fist.
This spot's got jokes and tales to share,
With every breeze, I chuckle in the air.

Old shoes hang from rusty nails,
The wind tells stories, and never fails.
In the distance, a lawnmower roars,
It's just my neighbor, house full of chores.

So here I sit, with laughter near,
In this place where silence cheers.
A hammock swings with a creaky sound,
In solitude's charm, I'm humor-bound.

Where Time Takes a Breath

Tick-tock seems to take a nap,
As I sip tea from my worn-out cap.
Clouds drift by like cotton candy,
Surrounded by plants, both lush and dandy.

My shoes are off, two socks in tow,
One's striped, the other? A no-show.
Birds are chirping a quirky tune,
While I serenade with a plastic spoon.

A chipmunk stops, checks out my snack,
He seems to have no sense of lack.
With chuckles shared beneath the trees,
We trade old jokes with the buzzing bees.

Here in this spot where time's absurd,
Every moment's just plain unheard.
In this laughter-laden, sunny space,
I find my joy, my happy place.

Echoes of Renewal

The old swing creaks, the memories flow,
Of days when we fought with water, a show.
With splashes and giggles, we'd dance in glee,
While the world was busy, we'd just be free.

An ice cream truck's jingle calls from afar,
Just a plump raccoon, oh, what a star!
He's dancing in rhythm, stealing my treats,
While I holler jokes and compete with his feats.

The flowers laugh as they bloom in roll,
Every petal's a tickle, a joy to the soul.
In the quiet moments, I find a spark,
Sowing seeds of laughter in daylight's park.

These echoes ring, a soft, sweet sound,
Where every chuckle is tightly wound.
With each passing breeze, I'm healed in part,
In these funny moments, I reclaim my heart.

The Gateway to Peace

A pot of thyme sings a fragrant tune,
While my chair rocks gently, oh how it swoons.
A ladybug winks, with a proud little strut,
Reminding me gently, life's just one big cut.

The neighbor's dog grumbles, chasing its tail,
While I sit and ponder my next baked sale.
My plants have stories, hard to believe,
Each leaf a chapter, a humorous reprieve.

A breeze whispers secrets of everyday bliss,
Like how shiny gnomes never want to miss.
In this nook of giggles, I'm never alone,
With whispers of nature, I find my tone.

From sunlit corners, joy spills and flows,
In this tiny haven where laughter grows.
So here I lounge, on this sunny lease,
Finding humor in life, my gateway to peace.

Tea and Thoughts in Abandon

A kettle whistles, tea's on track,
My cat's the judge, I smile back.
Sips of warmth, they fill the air,
With giggles bubbling, without a care.

Chairs creak softly, tales unfold,
Of ghosts that dance, both brave and bold.
Lemon drops and honey flows,
Sugar dreams in sunny throes.

Breezes carry laughter light,
As thoughts take off like birds in flight.
The world outside feels far away,
While silliness holds court today.

As blossoms bloom where laughter thrives,
We weave our joys in jiving dives.
So pour the tea, let worries fade,
In silly moments, memories made.

Echoes of Yesterday's Joy

In old rocking chairs, we sway and sway,
Hunting memories, come what may.
A funny tale from "back in the day,"
Made gramps snort tea, in a wild display.

The swing set creaks, though no one's there,
But ghosts of laughter fill the air.
Kickin' it back, like pirates bold,
With stories spun, like yarns of old.

Sunset hues dance on the porch,
As joy takes over, like a charming torch.
We giggle at crumbs from dinner past,
And raise a toast, our shadows cast.

Echoes linger in twilight's glow,
With nonsense rhymes that just won't go.
In every chuckle, love comes near,
In simple moments, we find our cheer.

Breathe, Believe, Be

Gazing out where flowers bloom,
I sip my drink, embrace the room.
With butterflies flitting, I giggle bright,
In the chaos of day, I breathe in light.

Thoughts like feathers, drift in sway,
As I trust in nonsense, come what may.
"Believe," I say, to the daffodil,
While ants hold meetings, oh what a thrill!

Twilight whispers, with frogs on cue,
A hilarious chant, join me too!
The world spins fast, but here I stay,
In funny little moments, come and play.

We twirl through dreams till night takes hold,
In giggles and chuckles, our hearts unfold.
Oh, breathe, believe, my friend, you see,
Life's sweet, absurd, just let it be!

Stories Woven in Silence

In quietude, where laughter sparks,
I find the joy in tiny quirks.
A bird takes flight, a wink from fate,
As humor weaves through moments late.

Beside me sits a tired shoe,
With stories shared, between me and you.
Tickling giggles from mossy spaces,
Hideaway smiles on silly faces.

Stray cats pounce in stealthy leaps,
While memories bubble, like oceans deep.
The wind's a jester, as shadows dance,
With silly thoughts that sing and prance.

Even in silence, tales unfold,
Of turtles slow and puppies bold.
In every wink of sunset's shade,
We find the joy that life had made.

In the Midst of Greenery

In the shade of leaves so lush,
Sipping lemonade, we laugh and hush,
A squirrel scampers, eyes on our treat,
While chair springs creak with every seat.

Birds chirp gossip, what a commotion,
While grasshoppers join in the notion,
That all our worries can just take flight,
As we revel in this pure delight.

Add a few ants with a dance routine,
They waddle in lines, oh so serene,
We hoot and holler, tossed with glee,
Who knew insects could bring us esprit!

So here we linger, carefree and bright,
In this patch of joy, all feels just right,
With laughter echoing through the air,
Our hearts as light as the breeze we share.

Beyond the Threshold of Worry

Just past the door, a world so free,
Where laughter escapes like buzzing bees,
With cookies baked and tea on the pot,
Each worry shrinks, what a pleasant lot!

Cushions piled, a fortress made,
Where laughter echoes, fears do fade,
With tales of mishaps and goofy flops,
We giggle till the coffee stops.

A cat wanders by, tail held high,
Chasing shadows as friends nearby,
They throw popcorn, share a big grin,
Who knew that joy could start from within?

So we're here, with stories to share,
In the glow of friendship, love in the air,
Tripping on laughs, oh what a thrill,
Beyond that door, we've found our chill.

Conversations Over Tea

In the age-old ritual, teacups gleam,
Pouring warmth, we stir and beam,
With each sip, a giggle slips,
As we navigate these fun-filled trips.

Rumors of neighbors, do you hear that?
The one with the hat, what's up with that?
We slosh our cups, spilling tales of cheer,
As laughter bubbles, our worries disappear.

"Did you hear about the dog on a quest?"
"A mailman chased him, that's quite a jest!"
We dive into stories so wild and wide,
With warmth of tea, our hearts open wide.

So here we sit, with voices raised,
In this gathering, we are all praised,
For in this moment, nothing feels wrong,
Just tea, and laughter, and friendship strong.

A Refuge for the Soul

Beneath the awning, we sit side by side,
With ice cream cones, we melt with pride,
As ants play tag upon our shoes,
Finding joy in the silliest news.

Weather's a buzzkill, but we don't mind,
We laugh at clouds, oh so unrefined,
With wit as sharp as a summer's breeze,
We outsmart gloom with the greatest of ease.

Meanwhile, birds do their best stand-up show,
With chirps and flaps, putting on a glow,
The world keeps turning, but we just stay,
In this fortress of fun, come what may.

So let's keep laughing, forget the fuss,
Our sanctuary, the two of us,
With joy sprouting like flowers in bloom,
We find solace in this vibrant room.

A Pathway to Still Waters

A cat on the railing, dreaming of heights,
Squirrels are staging their daring antics.
They hop and they twirl, what a silly sight,
While I sip my tea, my thoughts grow frantic.

The sun beats down like a drummer on crack,
Bees buzzing by like they're lost at a show.
I wave at my neighbor, she waves with a snack,
We laugh at our worries—what a strange flow!

The dog tries to chase the breeze with a bark,
While ducks leave quacks in the air like a tune.
A whimsical dance from morning till dark,
Awakening laughter beneath the bright moon.

So here on my seat, in this carnival space,
I find my joy in the commotion and fun.
Life's silly moments are a warm embrace,
Turning mundane hours into playful runs.

The Heartbeat of Serenity

A chair on the porch, where the sun likes to nap,
I'm knitting a story with yarn and some laughs.
A crow yells nonsense, wearing a black cap,
While squirrels debate their acorn-rich paths.

The mailman arrives like he's struck by a spell,
With packages dancing in circles around.
He trips on a hose, oh what luck! Oh well,
Coffee's on hold—it's a great day, I found!

My friend drops by with a hat on her cat,
She claims that it's fancy, a true regal crown.
The cat glares in silence, what's up with that?
While giggles escape, turning frowns upside down.

In this space of comfort, where quirks come alive,
I cherish the moments of laughter and zest.
With each sunny hour, my spirits do thrive,
Finding joy in mishaps, they bring out my best.

Visions of Serenity's Canvas

Picture this scene: a chair with a view,
A butterfly lands with a wobble and swirl.
I wink at the clouds floating soft and askew,
They giggle back down, giving nature a whirl.

The dog tries to woo me with a stick that he found,
He dances around, oh what a funny sight!
I toss it aside, he looks so profound,
Claiming this prize as his victory rite.

Neighbors stroll by, their laughter rings clear,
One claims that her garden is taking a leap!
But weeds in the flowerbeds manifest fear,
We giggle and joke, while the sun starts to creep.

Dusk falls upon us and shadows take flight,
Fireflies start winking like stars on the ground.
We chuckle at quirks, what a wonderful night,
In this quirky haven, true joy can be found.

Nature's Gentle Embrace

A swing on the porch, squeaks like a song,
Birds chirp in rhythm, trying to compete.
The wind joins in, playful all day long,
Crafting a choir that's silly and sweet.

A raccoon shimmies, stealing my snacks,
While ants do their tango, a parade of their own.
The flowers beside me, all wobbly like hacks,
Join in the fiesta, joyous and shown.

An ice cream truck rolls by with a jingle so bright,
The kids in the yard rush out with a cheer.
But I eye the old man who's ready to fight,
Over chocolate sprinkles, oh what a sphere!

Here on this porch, laughter dances and flits,
With each playful moment, joy we embrace.
Life's silly antics, like jigsaw pieces fit,
Nature's sweet humor, our favorite place.

Reflections in a Quiet Corner

In a nook where the cat naps,
And the cushions embrace the sun,
I sip on my tea, spilling dreams,
While the blender sings just for fun.

A squirrel thinks it's a raccoon,
As it steals crumbs from my shoe,
Laughing at its goofy dance,
I wonder if it's seen a zoo.

The plants chatter in hushed tones,
Debating the height of the grass,
While I join in with a wink,
As if nature has time to pass.

A moth casts shadows in twilight,
Trying to do the cha-cha slide,
And I, with popcorn in hand,
Join the fun from the porch side.

The Sanctuary of Stillness

In a realm where the wind whispers,
And the sun plays peek-a-boo,
I tell secrets to the daisies,
While they giggle, fresh with dew.

A chipmunk steals my sandwich,
Thinking it's his lucky day,
I can't help but chuckle loud,
As he scampers away.

The rocking chair holds my laugh,
As it creaks a funny tune,
While mockingbirds join the chorus,
Underneath the lazy moon.

The breeze brings a tickling touch,
And my hair starts to dance with glee,
Who knew stillness could be silly?
Only in this space, carefree.

Gentle Moments Unwound

Here's the tale of my old shoe,
It sprawls by the garden's door,
Claiming it's the king of comfort,
While my toes cry out for more!

A butterfly winks from the flower,
As if sharing a little joke,
I laugh at the way it flutters,
Like it's never felt a poke.

The wind swirls around my chair,
Like it's part of some grand team,
It puts on a gusty performance,
As I settle in with a dream.

Clouds giggle at their own shapes,
They morph into castles and fish,
I snort at their whimsy and jest,
In this healing where laughter is rich.

Hearth of Heartstrings

In a corner, a fire flickers,
Sending sparks like tiny stars,
Each crackle tells a wild story,
While I sit counting the jars.

The dog snores in comical rhythms,
As if leading a band of dreams,
His tail wagging in soft beats,
Creating a symphony of schemes.

Squirrels hold acorn meetings,
In the oak, bold and spry,
I whisper to them of adventure,
As they roll their eyes and fly.

The day bids a cheeky farewell,
With shadows dancing in the night,
I toast to the laughter here,
In this hearth, everything feels right.

The Resting Place of Dreams

In a chair that's lost its stride,
I find the world swaying wide.
A cat leaps in with a cushy pounce,
Now I know I've found my bounce.

A breeze comes by with a playful tease,
Whispers secrets through the trees.
Laughter echoes, a joyful sound,
In this spot, happiness is found.

With lemonade that dances sweet,
And squirrels that play hide and seek.
Dreams bounce like the sun's bright rays,
In this quirky resting place.

So here's to naps and giggles galore,
Where time stands still, and spirits soar!
A sanctuary beneath the sky,
Where worries dissipate and fly.

Sips of Comfort and Memories

With a cup of tea perched high,
I ponder life, oh me, oh my!
The world spins 'round like a dizzy dance,
As I spill some sweet on my pants.

Cookies crumbly, spilling cheer,
I chuckle loud, inviting near.
Friends gather with stories to share,
Each one funnier, without a care.

We sip and laugh 'til the sun goes down,
With tea stains as our only crown.
Memories bloom like flowers bright,
In this spot, everything feels right.

So raise your cup, let's toast away,
To silly moments that make our day!
In this serene and steady cheer,
Laughter lingers with those held dear.

A Place to Just Be

In a hammock that sways like it's dreaming,
I find peace, my soul beaming.
The world rushes past with its heavy chase,
While I sit here, enjoying the space.

Birds hold concerts, they sing with glee,
Their tunes dance around, wild and free.
I wave at clouds, they wave back slow,
This little spot, my happy meadow.

No rush to leave, no need to flee,
Just soaking in all that's meant to be.
The sun dips low, a golden hue,
In this place, life feels brand new.

So let the world whirl and spin away,
In my nest, I simply hay.
With laughter thumping in my chest,
Here's to being, it's the very best.

Healing Hands of Nature

In the garden where the daisies wave,
I dig my hands in, feeling brave.
A mud pie here, a flower there,
The earth grins wide, without a care.

Butterflies dance like silly fools,
While I dig up all the garden tools.
With dirt on my nose and joy all around,
Nature chuckles, without a sound.

Rain drops fall like tiny cheers,
Splashing joy, washing away fears.
In between giggles and innocent play,
Nature's hands guide me on my way.

So let my heart be light and free,
In nature's arms, I find the key.
Together we laugh, together we bloom,
In this funny, joyful, healing room.

Journeys Unseen from the Railings

From the railings, I can spy,
A squirrel stealing my french fry.
It's a culinary crime, I swear,
But he's cute, so I just stare.

The neighbors argue over their plants,
I think they're both wearing slants.
Their dogs bark like they're in a race,
While I sip tea at my own pace.

The postman slips, trips on my shoe,
Knocks over my gnome, oh boo-hoo!
He waves, his face a bright shade of red,
I chuckle, "Next time, watch where you tread!"

Chairs creak like a horror film's start,
With every squeak, it steals my heart.
I ponder life while birds take flight,
Ah, but those fries are out of sight!

The Sigh of Rest

With a sigh that could shake the clouds,
I plop down while the world crowds.
A cat leaps up, gives me a glare,
I guess my spot was 'reserved' there.

My lawn chair squeaks, a fitting tune,
To the laughter of kids in the afternoon.
Ice cream drips, a crazy mishap,
But it's summertime, so I just clap!

Neighbors laugh, they cook their meats,
While I'm here dodging sticky sweets.
Oh, to lounge without a care,
While my neighbor's grill lets out smoke in the air.

As twilight falls, I hear a whoosh,
A rogue frisbee, a youthful swoosh.
But I'm safe here, my drink right by,
Just me, the stars, and a lazy sigh.

Finding Peace in the Ordinary

I seek peace between the cracks,
Where garden gnomes hold secret acts.
The hose lies coiled, like a long snake,
But I just laugh and sip my cake.

The neighbors argue about the noise,
While I watch ants play with their toys.
A random breeze brings me a dream,
That life, my friends, isn't as it seems.

Laundry flutters like flags on display,
I'm a politician in my own way.
The cat rolls over, claiming my chair,
With her nose in the air, she has no care.

So here's to finding peace each day,
In ordinary things, come what may.
A puzzle piece in a comic book show,
Life's funny bits balance the woe.

Dreaming on the Edge of Night

As night creeps close, I dream in part,
A raccoon plays the piano, quite the art!
The moon winks down, a sly old chap,
Saying, "Keep dreaming, take a nap."

A firefly dances, it's quite absurd,
Saying, "Catch me if you can!" not a word.
With marshmallow clouds, I drift away,
Into funny lands where giggles sway.

The stars join in, they twinkle and tease,
As they waltz with shadows on the trees.
Here's a tale of squirrels with a band,
Rocking out with sticks in their hand.

So in the night, with laughter so bright,
I cherish these dreams till morning light.
For every chuckle beneath the sky,
Turns ordinary nights into a why!

Gentle Breezes and Kindred Spirits

A chair that wobbles welcomes all,
A squirrel's dance, it provides a haul.
With lemonade sips and tales absurd,
We laugh until our voices are blurred.

Each breeze that tickles our lazy feet,
Brings jokes from friends, oh what a treat!
A cat's smug face, perched up high,
As it plots to swipe the treats nearby.

The ants march on, a tiny parade,
With crumbs of snacks, their plans are laid.
In shade we gather, gossip and sigh,
While the sun sets low in a peachy sky.

So here we sit, with nature's cheer,
With jokes and laughter that we hold dear.
A knotted hammock, a sunflower too,
The breezes and friends, forever true.

The Refuge of a Gentle Dawn

Morning light peeks through a crack,
As roosters squawk, they'll get no slack.
We sip our coffee, laughter spills,
With sleepy eyes and shaky thrills.

The dog joins in, with wiggles galore,
Chasing the sunbeams across the floor.
A day of mischief lies ahead,
With plans that dance in each sleepy head.

Oops! A spill of milk on my dress,
Giggling fits, what a lovely mess!
The neighbors peek, with curious eyes,
As pancakes tumble, but who can disguise?

Now off we go, into the day,
With a grin on our faces, come what may.
With each silly moment, we surely find,
Our refuge in laughter, forever kind.

Stories Weave in the Fading Light

As stars appear, we gather round,
With stories silly, warmth is found.
In shadows dancing, tall tales rise,
Even Bigfoot can't hide from our eyes!

A moth buzzes, with swagger and glee,
Dancing too close to the old oak tree.
Ghosts of stories in laughter shake,
With every chuckle, the night feels great.

The fire crackles, its glow so bright,
As whispers float like dreams tonight.
Our laughter echoes, a wondrous tune,
Under the gaze of the questioning moon.

In fading light, the magic stirs,
With mischief lurking, just like the furs.
With every tale, our spirits lift,
In this secret world, a cherished gift.

Conversations with the Moon

The moon peeks down, with a cheeky grin,
Listening close to our chattering din.
We share our secrets, silly and bright,
"Don't eat too much, you'll hug the night!"

Cats plot and scheme, under starry space,
While crickets chirp with natural grace.
We toast with drinks, homemade and wild,
And discuss why grown-ups are always riled.

The air is thick with giggles and sighs,
As dreams flutter like fireflies in the skies.
A moonlit dance on the grass, so free,
Makes us believe in the magic we see.

With every glance up at the sparkling light,
We revel in joy, what a splendid sight!
For in these moments, we can't help but zoom,
In this delightful chat with the mischievous moon.

A Gentle Whisper Among Leaves

Leaves rustle softly, secrets shared,
The branches giggle, no need to be scared.
Squirrels play cards, in a wild game,
While the sun peeks in, never feeling lame.

A breeze takes a sip from my cool drink,
As shadows dance, making me think.
What if the trees throw a party tonight?
With acorns as snacks, oh, what a delight!

Birds bring the tunes with a jazzy flair,
While bugs tap their feet, floating in air.
Each branch a stage, each twig a throne,
Nature's wild laughter, a whimsical tone.

So I sit back, let the laughter grow,
In this leafy realm, where joy overflows.
With a gentle whisper, my cares disappear,
In this merry nook, life feels so sincere.

Nature's Song of Restoration

The flowers gossip, all colors aligned,
They share their gossip—what a good find!
The daisies are laughing at the snails' slow race,
While bees buzz around, sporting golden lace.

A tortoise in shades, sipping on dew,
Complains about age, but has stories too.
Nature chuckles, rolls over in glee,
As critters join in, oh, what a spree!

The sun plays games, hiding and peeking,
While shadows stretch long, and the creek's seeking.
Frogs croak their jokes, loud and free,
Creating a symphony, just for me.

So I rest on my spot, with thoughts light as air,
In this quirky concert, there's joy to spare.
With vibrant tunes in this green jubilee,
Life's silly harmony, it's just meant to be.

Hidden Nooks of Tranquility

In the secret corners where sunlight strays,
Lizards do cartwheels, in their funny ways.
An old bench sits, its paint peeling bright,
With whispers of stories in morning light.

A chipmunk appears with a nut in its cheek,
Squirrels laugh hard at the strange physique.
They play hide and seek among leaves and bark,
Nature's own antics—meeting, remark.

Butterflies twirl in a ballet of flight,
While flowers giggle, oh, what a sight!
The breeze has a chuckle, tickles my nose,
In the hidden nooks, anything goes.

I sit back and smile, with a drink in my hand,
As the world spins in laughter, so playful and grand.
In this sweet haven, where peace comes to play,
Each moment a treasure, come join the fray!

The Balmy Embrace of Night

The moon drapes a blanket, soft and serene,
As fireflies flicker, a dazzling sheen.
Crickets compose tunes, with rhythm and cheer,
Night's cool embrace, of laughter we hear.

Stars waltz above, with twinkling delight,
While owls crack wise, 'bout the day and its plight.
The shadows stretch tall, with a silly sway,
As nature indulges in nonsense and play.

A raccoon in shades looks quite out of place,
Stealing my snacks, with a sly, cheeky face.
The night air whispers jokes wrapped in mist,
In this lively scene, it's pure joy that persists.

So I lean back and chuckle, what a fine night,
Beneath giggling stars, feeling just right.
In the balmy embrace, my laughter takes flight,
As nature's own jesters perform in moonlight.

Whispers of Renewal

On a rickety chair, I sat with a grin,
My cat schemed and plotted, ready to win.
Each creak of the wood, a laugh in disguise,
As the sun whispered secrets, oh how time flies.

A squirrel made a dive for an acorn in flight,
I nearly fell off, but it felt just right.
The breeze tickled cheeks, a giggle escaped,
In the laughter of nature, my worries were draped.

Neighbors walked by with their own tales to tell,
While I sipped my drink, it all tasted swell.
As the butterflies danced through the warm air,
I chuckled aloud, deeply free of despair.

From shadows of doubts to bright beams of cheer,
My makeshift throne sparkled, no room for fear.
With each silly moment that life seemed to bring,
The joy of the little things made my heart sing.

A Seat Beneath the Stars

A folding chair waits, dressed in delight,
As I plop in with snacks, what a funny sight!
Crickets in chorus, the night air alive,
Each enigmatic croak helps my laughter thrive.

When the moon peeks in with a glimmer and grin,
My snack bag spills—oh lord, where to begin?
Stars giggle soft as they wink from the sky,
While the dog snuffles crumbs, oh my, oh my!

Cousins tell stories, some wild and bizarre,
About those ghosts lurking, just past the old car.
With a howl from the wolves, all giggles unfold,
Who knew that old legends could be so bold?

As we sit in a bunch, sharing joy and surprise,
The universe chuckles, its twinkle our prize.
In our laughter, the cosmos felt close and near,
A night full of whimsy, we've nothing to fear.

Nature's Embrace at Dusk

At dusk, the world shifts, painted in gold,
On my porch, with snacks, tales brave and bold.
The leaves tell a story, rustling with glee,
As the sun bids adieu with a wink just for me.

A bird dropped its dinner, an olive-soaked jest,
I laughed so hard, my old heart felt blessed.
Each sip of sweet tea carried whispers of fun,
While shadows danced lightly beneath the last sun.

The firefly conference, blinking like mad,
Exploded my thoughts, oh, why was I sad?
A ladybug climbed on my nose for a ride,
And the chuckles of nature swelled up deep inside.

As the sky turned to velvet, a soft blanket spread,
I giggled at moments that danced in my head.
With the moon's gentle giggle and stars all aglow,
Life's best little treasures are best shared below.

Gathering Light and Laughter

In the hazy dawn light, with coffee in hand,
The world looks so silly, a whimsical band.
The garden gnomes chuckle, their eyes full of tricks,
While the slugs contemplate, oh how they pick!

Birds gather round, orchestrating the day,
Cawing out laughter, they sing it my way.
The sun peeks through clouds, a spotlight on me,
As I bust out my dance, no one else can see!

My sandals are mismatched—what a fashion faux pas,
But with each goofy step, I'm a superstar!
The flowers all nod in a colorful cheer,
While the breeze whispers softly, "Just enjoy, my dear!"

At day's end, I'll sip on my favorite brew,
And tell stories to stars, both old and new.
In this joyful embrace, I share in delight,
Gathering laughter, from morning till night.

Footsteps in the Quiet

At dusk, the crickets tune their song,
While I search for my shoes that seem so wrong.
Wobbly chairs creak like they have a tale,
Of mischief managed, like the cat we all hail.

The neighbor's dog joins with a hearty bark,
As I chase the shadows creeping in the dark.
An ice cream cone melts faster than I run,
Sticky fingers giggling, oh what fun!

The breeze whispers secrets, I think I'm mad,
When squirrels knock over pots, oh, what a lad!
I plant my feet, and slip right off the seat,
In this little chaos, life feels so sweet.

So dance on the steps, oh what a show,
With laughter's echo, let the good times flow.
For in silly moments, joy will ignite,
Throughout our adventures in fading light.

Embracing the Golden Hour

As sunbeams sprinkle on our tangled tresses,
Where grass stains mark the silliest messes.
A sunhat flies off as I join the race,
And my chicken dance brightens every face.

The lemonade stands are quite the delight,
With a splash of joy, not a hint of fright.
My friend spills his drink, oh what a scene,
While ants applaud our summer routine.

A picnic blanket, our fortress of fun,
As we plot adventures, laughter's begun.
We toss the frisbee, it wanders away,
To find it in bushes—where did it stray?

With each sunset glow, a memory locked,
In our hearts like treasure, never docked.
We savor the silly, each moment divine,
In our golden hour, our souls intertwine.

Where Time Stands Still

Tick-tock on the clock, but who cares to know?
When cupcakes and giggles put on quite the show!
A comic book page is the new scene we make,
As time laughs at plans we just can't shake.

Old chairs, they sway under all of our weight,
As we ponder the meaning of birthday cake fate.
With crumbs on our chins, we plan our escape,
To lands made of pudding and blanket escape.

The world outside hums like a busy bee,
But here on our porch, there's just you and me.
With puns and pitter-patter, the moments unfold,
In the treasure of laughter that never grows old.

So let whispers of tales and giggles collide,
In a place where no hurry or worry can hide.
For every tick, we counter with glee,
In our timeless realm, just you and me.

Echoes of Laughter and Love

In the early dawn, we share sleepy eyes,
Where pancakes and syrup win breakfast prize.
My brother flips flapjacks, oh what a mess,
With giggles so loud, who needs a dress?

A game of charades, all pokes and flails,
When my dad acts as fish; he's got no scales.
We roar with delight as he tries to swim,
All while grandma snickers, her humor a whim.

Outside the world spins, but here we plant roots,
In laughter that fills our worn-out boots.
With every "remember when," our spirits shall sing,
We keep love alive, the joy that we bring.

So raise your glass high, toast to the fun,
As echoes of laughter keep us forever young.
In heartbeats of friendship, we find our song,
In sweet moments shared, where we all belong.

www.ingramcontent.com/pod-product-compliance
Lightning Source LLC
Chambersburg PA
CBHW051729290426
43661CB00122B/139